To Miko with Love
A.K.

For information about creative music - movement - art book series visit www.artskindred.com

Written by: Anetta Kotowicz
Illustrated by: Nina Ezhik
Graphic Concept and Art Direction by: Anetta Kotowicz
Edited by: Anita Bushell

New York - 2018
Library of Congress Control Number: 2018907334

Hardcover ISBN: 978-1-7321862-3-1

How to find songs and music?
Subscribe to YouTube channel: Arts Kindred Magic,
and select the Winter Song playlist
or scan the code below

SCAN ME!

Requires QR Code Reader App
and Internet Connection

To purchase the Winter Songs music album visit
www.ArtsKindred.com

A Day in the Life of a Kid:

WinteR SonG

written by Anetta Kotowicz
illustrated by Nina Ezhik

artskindred
2018 New York

Every season has music
Every season shares joy
Every season sounds with colors

Can you hear it?

It's time to explore!

Good morning, Billy Bear,
Are you ready for a walk?
Let's find out what is waiting
For us, right there - outside!

It is cloudy, it is cold,
Our home is cozy and warm!
We are waiting patiently,
The magic will start soon…

Get your sweater and your snow pants,
Take your mittens, scarf, and hat,
Warmest jacket and big snow boots,
Winter's cold – We all know that!

Come outside and play with me today,
Come outside and play with me!
Winter has a **magic charm**,
We will have a joyful time.

Look and listen! It's so silent...
Tiny snowflakes fall around,

Whirling, twirling

very lightly,

'Till they gently

touch the ground.

Lightly **whirl and twirl,**
Sing a joyful Ding-Dong-Ding!
Lightly **whirl and twirl,**
Let the winter season sing!

Snowballs falling **POP-POP! POP-POP!**
Snowball fight! Get ready, start!
Make a snowball, toss it far,
It must reach the other side!

POP-POP! POP-POP! Whirl and twirl,
Sing a joyful Ding-Dong-Ding!
POP-POP! POP-POP! Whirl and twirl,
Let the winter season sing!

Look and listen!

Hear the sparkle,

Pointy icicles play along!

Winter sun rays magic music:

Ding-dong,

Ding-dong,

Ding-Dong Song!

DING-DONG!

Whirl and twirl,
Sing a joyful Ding-Dong-Ding!

DING-DONG!

Whirl and twirl,
Let the winter season sing!

Time to   walk with   friends to - ge - ther

stomp   stomp   stomp stomp   stomp stomp stomp   stomp

Throw some   snowballs   in such   weather

pop-pop   pop-pop   pop-pop   pop-pop

Roll   a   big one,   medium,   small

R o - o - o - o l l

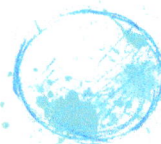

Roll

Watch the   snowman   growing   tall!

Is that all?
Oh, no!

Eyes and  nose and  smile and  buttons,

pat-pat   pat-pat   pat-pat   pat-pat

Hat and  scarf, some  magic   dust

sprinkle   sprinkle   sprinkle   sprinkle

Pop-pop!   Wheeee!   and   Jin-gle-ing

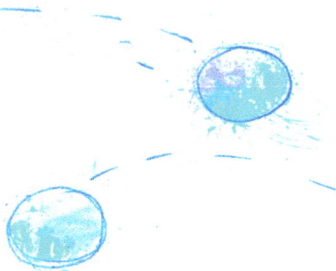  

Let the winter season sing!

Look up now! On the snowy tree,
A few little red birds
Are chirping at me:

Chirp-chirp, chirp-chirp,
We have some hungry bellies,
Chirp-chirp, chirp-chirp,
No seeds, no yummy berries!

Don't forget to feed us
In the winter time,
And we will sing a song for you
When **spring** will come!

Look and listen!
Winter's calling
Horses pull the **jingling** sled,
Hear the smiles and joyful voices,
Winter music in my head!

Look and listen!

Winter's calling

Be my helpers, everyone!

Bake the cookies, set the tables,

Share the stories

from near and far!

In the silence of a snowy day,
Trees and buildings, stars above,
Brilliant lights shine all around,
Spreading kindness, peace and love!

Candlelight,

shining bright,
Sparkling peaceful light,

Candlelight,

shining bright,
Warming every heart,

Stars above,

help me shine,
just like the

Candlelight,

shining bright...

Party time!

We share our cookies,
Sip delicious hot cocoa,
Looking at the whisper
               of the snow
We sing the winter's song.

What song?

Lightly whirl and twirl,
Sing a joyful **Ding-Dong-Ding!**
Lightly whirl and twirl,
Let the winter season sing!

Would you like to play games?

Flip this page...

SURPRISE!

Let's play!

Note about the board game:
- the best way to play is by enlarging it
- game instructions on the last page of the book

LOOK:

Find these crafts in our book, just flip the pages and look again.
Make your own crafts!

*make festive chains
with your drawings
on colored paper and
attach them to
the string or ribbon*

*slices of dried oranges, pinecones,
anise stars, cinnamon sticks
cranberries or popcorn on the strings,
make great smelling ornaments*

*simple lantern,
made by decorating
a glass jar*

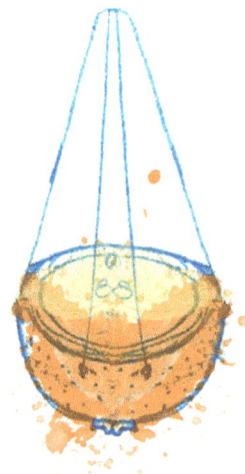

*bird friendly feeder - like this,
holding seeds mixed with a touch
of oil, made of an orange peel*

LISTEN:

Find the Winter Song playlist on the Arts Kindred Magic YouTube channel.
Let's listen to the music, looking at corresponding pages in this book!
Look at the pictures above. Where is the jingle bell, triangle, tambourine,
chimes bar, glockenspiel and bongos and big cymbals?
Arts Kindred Magic app will help you learn sounds of these instruments.
Listen to the Winter Music recording. Can you name all the instruments?

41
42
43
sleep 1 turn
44
45

Finish

Start

1

2

3

4

5

6

Climbing, climbing up the hill

Let's slide down on our backs!

Wheeee!

The ride goes   smooth and fast –

THUMP!

Can you   follow snowy tracks?

7

8

9

16
15
14
13
12
11
10

WINTER

is a wonderful time for listening to the stories from other cultures and countries. We can learn and share many traditions, customs and songs, just check the traditional eastern European cakes and cookies in our book!

We also like making outdoor decorations that birds and wildlife will enjoy. Later we can observe lots of prints in the snow and learn who visited us. How do you like to spend long winter's evenings?

HI! It's me, Pompon!

Did you read my Autumn Song? I hope you didn't miss it! I had so much fun exploring the autumn season. Can't wait to do it again with you!

Post your pictures @ArtsKindred #ArtsKindredMagic, #ADayInTheLifeOfAKid

WINTER GAME INSTRUCTIONS:

You need 1 pawn for each player and 1 die to share when taking turns,
or be creative and substitute these with easy-to-find objects - it's up to you!
(Ex. a die - you write numbers on a rubber eraser side,
as a pawn - use some small figures or blocks in different colors)

You'll also need an instrument - a bell. Don't worry if you don't have it!
How about finding something that makes the "right sound"?
Just look around - empty pots, metal bowls or buckets, some wooden spoons,
pot lids, they all work great!

Here is our bell - the jingle bell, but all bells are great!
Another choice: use our app to make sounds, but it's more fun with real instruments!

Start. Roll a die and move your pawn. Look where you landed.
Space with the bell? Make a bell concert and sing along if you like.
Space with animal tracks? Guess who left those tracks in the snow and move
around the room like your animal:

rabbit: reindeer: bird:

Don't forget to have a dance party on the finish line - and some snacks too!

ENJOY THE GAME!

www.ingramcontent.com/pod-product-compliance
Lightning Source LLC
Chambersburg PA
CBHW060753150426
42811CB00058B/1397

.